Gratitude Journal

The Adventures of SCUBA JACK

> "Piglet noticed that even though he had a Very Small Heart, it could hold a rather large amount of Gratitude."
> - A.A. Milne, Winnie-the-Pooh

What were the highlights of your week?

I AM THANKFUL FOR…   DATE:

1. _____

2. _____

3. _____

I AM THANKFUL FOR…   DATE:

1. _____

2. _____

3. _____

I AM THANKFUL FOR…   DATE:

1. _____

2. _____

3. _____

What were the highlights of your week?

I AM THANKFUL FOR...   DATE:

1. _____
2. _____
3. _____

I AM THANKFUL FOR...   DATE:

1. _____
2. _____
3. _____

I AM THANKFUL FOR...   DATE:

1. _____
2. _____
3. _____

I AM THANKFUL FOR...   DATE:

1. _____
2. _____
3. _____

> "Joy is really the simplest form of gratitude!"
> - Karl Barth

What were the highlights of your week?

I AM THANKFUL FOR...   DATE:

1. _____

2. _____

3. _____

I AM THANKFUL FOR...   DATE:

1. _____

2. _____

3. _____

I AM THANKFUL FOR...   DATE:

1. _____

2. _____

3. _____

What were the highlights of your week?

I AM THANKFUL FOR...   DATE:

1. _____
2. _____
3. _____

I AM THANKFUL FOR...   DATE:

1. _____
2. _____
3. _____

I AM THANKFUL FOR...   DATE:

1. _____
2. _____
3. _____

I AM THANKFUL FOR...   DATE:

1. _____
2. _____
3. _____

> "Feeling gratitude and not expressing it, is like wrapping a present and not giving it!"
> - William Arthur Ward

What were the highlights of your week?

I AM THANKFUL FOR...   DATE:

1. _____

2. _____

3. _____

I AM THANKFUL FOR...   DATE:

1. _____

2. _____

3. _____

I AM THANKFUL FOR...   DATE:

1. _____

2. _____

3. _____

What were the highlights of your week?

I AM THANKFUL FOR...   DATE:

1. _____

2. _____

3. _____

I AM THANKFUL FOR...   DATE:

1. _____

2. _____

3. _____

I AM THANKFUL FOR...   DATE:

1. _____

2. _____

3. _____

I AM THANKFUL FOR...   DATE:

1. _____

2. _____

3. _____

> "When we focus on our gratitude, the tide of disappointment goes out the and the tide of love rushes in."
> - Kristin Armstrong

What were the highlights of your week?

I AM THANKFUL FOR...   DATE:

1. _____

2. _____

3. _____

I AM THANKFUL FOR...   DATE:

1. _____

2. _____

3. _____

I AM THANKFUL FOR...   DATE:

1. _____

2. _____

3. _____

What were the highlights of your week?

I AM THANKFUL FOR...   DATE:

1. _____

2. _____

3. _____

I AM THANKFUL FOR...   DATE:

1. _____

2. _____

3. _____

I AM THANKFUL FOR...   DATE:

1. _____

2. _____

3. _____

I AM THANKFUL FOR...   DATE:

1. _____

2. _____

3. _____

> "When gratitude becomes an essential foundation in our lives, miracles start to appear everywhere!"
> - Emmanuel Dalgher

What were the highlights of your week?

I AM THANKFUL FOR…   DATE:

1. _____

2. _____

3. _____

I AM THANKFUL FOR…   DATE:

1. _____

2. _____

3. _____

I AM THANKFUL FOR…   DATE:

1. _____

2. _____

3. _____

What were the highlights of your week?

I AM THANKFUL FOR…   DATE:

1. _____

2. _____

3. _____

I AM THANKFUL FOR…   DATE:

1. _____

2. _____

3. _____

I AM THANKFUL FOR…   DATE:

1. _____

2. _____

3. _____

I AM THANKFUL FOR…   DATE:

1. _____

2. _____

3. _____

> "When I started counting my blessings, my whole life turned around."
> - Willie Nelson

What were the highlights of your week?

I AM THANKFUL FOR…   DATE:

1. _____

2. _____

3. _____

I AM THANKFUL FOR…   DATE:

1. _____

2. _____

3. _____

I AM THANKFUL FOR…   DATE:

1. _____

2. _____

3. _____

What were the highlights of your week?

I AM THANKFUL FOR...   DATE:

1. _____
2. _____
3. _____

I AM THANKFUL FOR...   DATE:

1. _____
2. _____
3. _____

I AM THANKFUL FOR...   DATE:

1. _____
2. _____
3. _____

I AM THANKFUL FOR...   DATE:

1. _____
2. _____
3. _____

> "No matter what language you speak, a kind and smiling "Thank You" always speaks to everyone's heart."
> - Roxana Jones

What were the highlights of your week?

I AM THANKFUL FOR...   DATE:

1. _____
2. _____
3. _____

I AM THANKFUL FOR...   DATE:

1. _____
2. _____
3. _____

I AM THANKFUL FOR...   DATE:

1. _____
2. _____
3. _____

What were the highlights of your week?

I AM THANKFUL FOR... DATE:

1. _____
2. _____
3. _____

I AM THANKFUL FOR... DATE:

1. _____
2. _____
3. _____

I AM THANKFUL FOR... DATE:

1. _____
2. _____
3. _____

I AM THANKFUL FOR... DATE:

1. _____
2. _____
3. _____

> "Gratitude helps us to see what is there instead of what isn't."
> - Annette Bridges

What were the highlights of your week?

I AM THANKFUL FOR...   DATE:

1. _____
2. _____
3. _____

I AM THANKFUL FOR...   DATE:

1. _____
2. _____
3. _____

I AM THANKFUL FOR...   DATE:

1. _____
2. _____
3. _____

What were the highlights of your week?

I AM THANKFUL FOR...   DATE:

1. _____
2. _____
3. _____

I AM THANKFUL FOR...   DATE:

1. _____
2. _____
3. _____

I AM THANKFUL FOR...   DATE:

1. _____
2. _____
3. _____

I AM THANKFUL FOR...   DATE:

1. _____
2. _____
3. _____

What were the highlights of your week?

I AM THANKFUL FOR...   DATE:

1. _____

2. _____

3. _____

I AM THANKFUL FOR...   DATE:

1. _____

2. _____

3. _____

I AM THANKFUL FOR...   DATE:

1. _____

2. _____

3. _____

What were the highlights of your week?

I AM THANKFUL FOR...   DATE:

1. _____
2. _____
3. _____

I AM THANKFUL FOR...   DATE:

1. _____
2. _____
3. _____

I AM THANKFUL FOR...   DATE:

1. _____
2. _____
3. _____

I AM THANKFUL FOR...   DATE:

1. _____
2. _____
3. _____

"To be grateful means to find blessings in everything!"

What were the highlights of your week?

I AM THANKFUL FOR...   DATE:

1. _____
2. _____
3. _____

I AM THANKFUL FOR...   DATE:

1. _____
2. _____
3. _____

I AM THANKFUL FOR...   DATE:

1. _____
2. _____
3. _____

What were the highlights of your week?

I AM THANKFUL FOR...   DATE:

1. _____
2. _____
3. _____

I AM THANKFUL FOR...   DATE:

1. _____
2. _____
3. _____

I AM THANKFUL FOR...   DATE:

1. _____
2. _____
3. _____

I AM THANKFUL FOR...   DATE:

1. _____
2. _____
3. _____

> "Gratitude can transform common days into Thanksgivings, turn routine jobs into joy, and change ordinary opportunities into blessings." - Annette Bridges

What were the highlights of your week?

I AM THANKFUL FOR...   DATE:

1. _____

2. _____

3. _____

I AM THANKFUL FOR...   DATE:

1. _____

2. _____

3. _____

I AM THANKFUL FOR...   DATE:

1. _____

2. _____

3. _____

What were the highlights of your week?

I AM THANKFUL FOR...   DATE:

1. _____

2. _____

3. _____

I AM THANKFUL FOR...   DATE:

1. _____

2. _____

3. _____

I AM THANKFUL FOR...   DATE:

1. _____

2. _____

3. _____

I AM THANKFUL FOR...   DATE:

1. _____

2. _____

3. _____

> "Whatever you appreciate and give thanks
> for will increase in your life!"
> - Sanaya Roman

What were the highlights of your week?

I AM THANKFUL FOR…   DATE:

1. _____

2. _____

3. _____

I AM THANKFUL FOR…   DATE:

1. _____

2. _____

3. _____

I AM THANKFUL FOR…   DATE:

1. _____

2. _____

3. _____

What were the highlights of your week?

I AM THANKFUL FOR…   DATE:

1. _____

2. _____

3. _____

I AM THANKFUL FOR…   DATE:

1. _____

2. _____

3. _____

I AM THANKFUL FOR…   DATE:

1. _____

2. _____

3. _____

I AM THANKFUL FOR…   DATE:

1. _____

2. _____

3. _____

> "Gratitude will shift you to a higher frequency, and you will attract much better things."
> - Rhonda Byrne

What were the highlights of your week?

I AM THANKFUL FOR…   DATE:

1. _____
2. _____
3. _____

I AM THANKFUL FOR…   DATE:

1. _____
2. _____
3. _____

I AM THANKFUL FOR…   DATE:

1. _____
2. _____
3. _____

What were the highlights of your week?

I AM THANKFUL FOR...   DATE:

1. _____

2. _____

3. _____

I AM THANKFUL FOR...   DATE:

1. _____

2. _____

3. _____

I AM THANKFUL FOR...   DATE:

1. _____

2. _____

3. _____

I AM THANKFUL FOR...   DATE:

1. _____

2. _____

3. _____

> "Life is full of give and take. Give thanks and
> Take nothing for Granted"
> - Scott Harris

What were the highlights of your week?

I AM THANKFUL FOR…   DATE:

1. _____
2. _____
3. _____

I AM THANKFUL FOR…   DATE:

1. _____
2. _____
3. _____

I AM THANKFUL FOR…   DATE:

1. _____
2. _____
3. _____

What were the highlights of your week?

I AM THANKFUL FOR… DATE:

1. _____
2. _____
3. _____

I AM THANKFUL FOR… DATE:

1. _____
2. _____
3. _____

I AM THANKFUL FOR… DATE:

1. _____
2. _____
3. _____

I AM THANKFUL FOR… DATE:

1. _____
2. _____
3. _____

> "The best time be grateful is always"
> - Buddha Groove

What were the highlights of your week?

I AM THANKFUL FOR...   DATE:

1. _____
2. _____
3. _____

I AM THANKFUL FOR...   DATE:

1. _____
2. _____
3. _____

I AM THANKFUL FOR...   DATE:

1. _____
2. _____
3. _____

What were the highlights of your week?

I AM THANKFUL FOR...   DATE:

1. _____
2. _____
3. _____

I AM THANKFUL FOR...   DATE:

1. _____
2. _____
3. _____

I AM THANKFUL FOR...   DATE:

1. _____
2. _____
3. _____

I AM THANKFUL FOR...   DATE:

1. _____
2. _____
3. _____

> "What a precious privilege it is to be alive
> - To breathe, to think, to enjoy, to love."
> - Marcus Aurelius

What were the highlights of your week?

I AM THANKFUL FOR...   DATE:

1. _____

2. _____

3. _____

I AM THANKFUL FOR...   DATE:

1. _____

2. _____

3. _____

I AM THANKFUL FOR...   DATE:

1. _____

2. _____

3. _____

What were the highlights of your week?

I AM THANKFUL FOR...   DATE:

1. _____

2. _____

3. _____

I AM THANKFUL FOR...   DATE:

1. _____

2. _____

3. _____

I AM THANKFUL FOR...   DATE:

1. _____

2. _____

3. _____

I AM THANKFUL FOR...   DATE:

1. _____

2. _____

3. _____

> "Create the highest, grandest version possible for your life, because you become what you believe."
> - Oprah Winfrey

What were the highlights of your week?

I AM THANKFUL FOR...   DATE:

1. _____
2. _____
3. _____

I AM THANKFUL FOR...   DATE:

1. _____
2. _____
3. _____

I AM THANKFUL FOR...   DATE:

1. _____
2. _____
3. _____

What were the highlights of your week?

I AM THANKFUL FOR...   DATE:

1. _____
2. _____
3. _____

I AM THANKFUL FOR...   DATE:

1. _____
2. _____
3. _____

I AM THANKFUL FOR...   DATE:

1. _____
2. _____
3. _____

I AM THANKFUL FOR...   DATE:

1. _____
2. _____
3. _____

> "You will never change your life until you change something you do daily. The secret of your success is found in your daily routine."   - Darren Hardy

What were the highlights of your week?

I AM THANKFUL FOR...   DATE:

1. _____
2. _____
3. _____

I AM THANKFUL FOR...   DATE:

1. _____
2. _____
3. _____

I AM THANKFUL FOR...   DATE:

1. _____
2. _____
3. _____

What were the highlights of your week?

I AM THANKFUL FOR...   DATE:

1. _____

2. _____

3. _____

I AM THANKFUL FOR...   DATE:

1. _____

2. _____

3. _____

I AM THANKFUL FOR...   DATE:

1. _____

2. _____

3. _____

I AM THANKFUL FOR...   DATE:

1. _____

2. _____

3. _____

> "When life gives you lemons, make orange juice and leave the world wondering how you did it."
> - Mitch Griego

What were the highlights of your week?

I AM THANKFUL FOR…   DATE:

1. _____
2. _____
3. _____

I AM THANKFUL FOR…   DATE:

1. _____
2. _____
3. _____

I AM THANKFUL FOR…   DATE:

1. _____
2. _____
3. _____

What were the highlights of your week?

I AM THANKFUL FOR...   DATE:

1. _____
2. _____
3. _____

I AM THANKFUL FOR...   DATE:

1. _____
2. _____
3. _____

I AM THANKFUL FOR...   DATE:

1. _____
2. _____
3. _____

I AM THANKFUL FOR...   DATE:

1. _____
2. _____
3. _____

> "Enjoy the little things, for one day you may look back and realize they were the big things."
> - Robert Brault

What were the highlights of your week?

I AM THANKFUL FOR...   DATE:

1. _____

2. _____

3. _____

I AM THANKFUL FOR...   DATE:

1. _____

2. _____

3. _____

I AM THANKFUL FOR...   DATE:

1. _____

2. _____

3. _____

What were the highlights of your week?

I AM THANKFUL FOR…   DATE:

1. _____

2. _____

3. _____

I AM THANKFUL FOR…   DATE:

1. _____

2. _____

3. _____

I AM THANKFUL FOR…   DATE:

1. _____

2. _____

3. _____

I AM THANKFUL FOR…   DATE:

1. _____

2. _____

3. _____

> "Be thankful for what you have; you'll end up having more. If you concentrate on what you don't have, you will never, ever have enough." - Oprah Winfrey

What were the highlights of your week?

I AM THANKFUL FOR...   DATE:

1. _____
2. _____
3. _____

I AM THANKFUL FOR...   DATE:

1. _____
2. _____
3. _____

I AM THANKFUL FOR...   DATE:

1. _____
2. _____
3. _____

What were the highlights of your week?

I AM THANKFUL FOR...   DATE:

1. _____

2. _____

3. _____

I AM THANKFUL FOR...   DATE:

1. _____

2. _____

3. _____

I AM THANKFUL FOR...   DATE:

1. _____

2. _____

3. _____

I AM THANKFUL FOR...   DATE:

1. _____

2. _____

3. _____

> "I looked around and thought about my life. I felt grateful. And I noticed every detail. That is the key to time travel. You can only move if you are actually in the moment. You have to be where you are to get where you need to go."   - Amy Poehler

What were the highlights of your week?

I AM THANKFUL FOR…   DATE:

1. _____

2. _____

3. _____

I AM THANKFUL FOR…   DATE:

1. _____

2. _____

3. _____

I AM THANKFUL FOR…   DATE:

1. _____

2. _____

3. _____

What were the highlights of your week?

I AM THANKFUL FOR…   DATE:

1. _____
2. _____
3. _____

I AM THANKFUL FOR…   DATE:

1. _____
2. _____
3. _____

I AM THANKFUL FOR…   DATE:

1. _____
2. _____
3. _____

I AM THANKFUL FOR…   DATE:

1. _____
2. _____
3. _____

> "The more grateful I am, the more beauty I see."
> - Mary Davis

What were the highlights of your week?

I AM THANKFUL FOR...   DATE:

1. _____

2. _____

3. _____

I AM THANKFUL FOR...   DATE:

1. _____

2. _____

3. _____

I AM THANKFUL FOR...   DATE:

1. _____

2. _____

3. _____

What were the highlights of your week?

I AM THANKFUL FOR…   DATE:

1. _____

2. _____

3. _____

I AM THANKFUL FOR…   DATE:

1. _____

2. _____

3. _____

I AM THANKFUL FOR…   DATE:

1. _____

2. _____

3. _____

I AM THANKFUL FOR…   DATE:

1. _____

2. _____

3. _____

> "Each day I am thankful for nights that turned into mornings, friends that turned into family, dreams that turned into reality, and likes that turned into love."
> - unknown

What were the highlights of your week?

I AM THANKFUL FOR...   DATE:

1. _____

2. _____

3. _____

I AM THANKFUL FOR...   DATE:

1. _____

2. _____

3. _____

I AM THANKFUL FOR...   DATE:

1. _____

2. _____

3. _____

What were the highlights of your week?

I AM THANKFUL FOR...   DATE:

1. _____
2. _____
3. _____

I AM THANKFUL FOR...   DATE:

1. _____
2. _____
3. _____

I AM THANKFUL FOR...   DATE:

1. _____
2. _____
3. _____

I AM THANKFUL FOR...   DATE:

1. _____
2. _____
3. _____

> "Happiness cannot be traveled to, owned, earned, worn or consumed. Happiness is the spiritual experience of living every minute with love, grace, & gratitude."
> - Denis Waitley

What were the highlights of your week?

I AM THANKFUL FOR…   DATE:

1. _____

2. _____

3. _____

I AM THANKFUL FOR…   DATE:

1. _____

2. _____

3. _____

I AM THANKFUL FOR…   DATE:

1. _____

2. _____

3. _____

What were the highlights of your week?

I AM THANKFUL FOR...   DATE:

1. _____
2. _____
3. _____

I AM THANKFUL FOR...   DATE:

1. _____
2. _____
3. _____

I AM THANKFUL FOR...   DATE:

1. _____
2. _____
3. _____

I AM THANKFUL FOR...   DATE:

1. _____
2. _____
3. _____

> "Remember that what you now have was once among the things you only hoped for"
> - Epicurus

What were the highlights of your week?

I AM THANKFUL FOR...   DATE:

1. _____
2. _____
3. _____

I AM THANKFUL FOR...   DATE:

1. _____
2. _____
3. _____

I AM THANKFUL FOR...   DATE:

1. _____
2. _____
3. _____

What were the highlights of your week?

I AM THANKFUL FOR...   DATE:

1. _____

2. _____

3. _____

I AM THANKFUL FOR...   DATE:

1. _____

2. _____

3. _____

I AM THANKFUL FOR...   DATE:

1. _____

2. _____

3. _____

I AM THANKFUL FOR...   DATE:

1. _____

2. _____

3. _____

> "Gratitude turns what we have into enough."
> - Melody Beattie

What were the highlights of your week?

I AM THANKFUL FOR...   DATE:

1. _____
2. _____
3. _____

I AM THANKFUL FOR...   DATE:

1. _____
2. _____
3. _____

I AM THANKFUL FOR...   DATE:

1. _____
2. _____
3. _____

What were the highlights of your week?

I AM THANKFUL FOR…   DATE:

1. _____

2. _____

3. _____

I AM THANKFUL FOR…   DATE:

1. _____

2. _____

3. _____

I AM THANKFUL FOR…   DATE:

1. _____

2. _____

3. _____

I AM THANKFUL FOR…   DATE:

1. _____

2. _____

3. _____

> "When we focus on our gratitude, the tide of disappointment goes out, and the tide of love rushes in."
> - Melody Beattie

What were the highlights of your week?

I AM THANKFUL FOR...   DATE:

1. _____

2. _____

3. _____

I AM THANKFUL FOR...   DATE:

1. _____

2. _____

3. _____

I AM THANKFUL FOR...   DATE:

1. _____

2. _____

3. _____

What were the highlights of your week?

I AM THANKFUL FOR...   DATE:

1. _____

2. _____

3. _____

I AM THANKFUL FOR...   DATE:

1. _____

2. _____

3. _____

I AM THANKFUL FOR...   DATE:

1. _____

2. _____

3. _____

I AM THANKFUL FOR...   DATE:

1. _____

2. _____

3. _____

What were the highlights of your week?

I AM THANKFUL FOR…   DATE:

1. _____

2. _____

3. _____

I AM THANKFUL FOR…   DATE:

1. _____

2. _____

3. _____

I AM THANKFUL FOR…   DATE:

1. _____

2. _____

3. _____

What were the highlights of your week?

I AM THANKFUL FOR...   DATE:

1. _____

2. _____

3. _____

I AM THANKFUL FOR...   DATE:

1. _____

2. _____

3. _____

I AM THANKFUL FOR...   DATE:

1. _____

2. _____

3. _____

I AM THANKFUL FOR...   DATE:

1. _____

2. _____

3. _____

> "We can only be said to be alive in those moments when our hearts are conscious of our treasures."
> - Thornton Wilder

What were the highlights of your week?

I AM THANKFUL FOR…   DATE:

1. _____

2. _____

3. _____

I AM THANKFUL FOR…   DATE:

1. _____

2. _____

3. _____

I AM THANKFUL FOR…   DATE:

1. _____

2. _____

3. _____

What were the highlights of your week?

I AM THANKFUL FOR...   DATE:

1. _____
2. _____
3. _____

I AM THANKFUL FOR...   DATE:

1. _____
2. _____
3. _____

I AM THANKFUL FOR...   DATE:

1. _____
2. _____
3. _____

I AM THANKFUL FOR...   DATE:

1. _____
2. _____
3. _____

> "It is not happy people who are thankful; it is thankful people who are happy."

What were the highlights of your week?

I AM THANKFUL FOR...   DATE:

1. _____

2. _____

3. _____

I AM THANKFUL FOR...   DATE:

1. _____

2. _____

3. _____

I AM THANKFUL FOR...   DATE:

1. _____

2. _____

3. _____

What were the highlights of your week?

I AM THANKFUL FOR...   DATE:

1. _____

2. _____

3. _____

I AM THANKFUL FOR...   DATE:

1. _____

2. _____

3. _____

I AM THANKFUL FOR...   DATE:

1. _____

2. _____

3. _____

I AM THANKFUL FOR...   DATE:

1. _____

2. _____

3. _____

> "Count your rainbows, not your thunderstorms"
> - Alyssa Knight

What were the highlights of your week?

I AM THANKFUL FOR...   DATE:

1. _____
2. _____
3. _____

I AM THANKFUL FOR...   DATE:

1. _____
2. _____
3. _____

I AM THANKFUL FOR...   DATE:

1. _____
2. _____
3. _____

What were the highlights of your week?

I AM THANKFUL FOR…   DATE:

1. _____

2. _____

3. _____

I AM THANKFUL FOR…   DATE:

1. _____

2. _____

3. _____

I AM THANKFUL FOR…   DATE:

1. _____

2. _____

3. _____

I AM THANKFUL FOR…   DATE:

1. _____

2. _____

3. _____

"To live with gratitude ever in our hearts is to touch heaven."
- Thomas S. Monson

What were the highlights of your week?

I AM THANKFUL FOR…   DATE:

1. _____

2. _____

3. _____

I AM THANKFUL FOR…   DATE:

1. _____

2. _____

3. _____

I AM THANKFUL FOR…   DATE:

1. _____

2. _____

3. _____

What were the highlights of your week?

I AM THANKFUL FOR...   DATE:

1. _____
2. _____
3. _____

I AM THANKFUL FOR...   DATE:

1. _____
2. _____
3. _____

I AM THANKFUL FOR...   DATE:

1. _____
2. _____
3. _____

I AM THANKFUL FOR...   DATE:

1. _____
2. _____
3. _____

"When you look at life through eyes of gratitude, the world becomes a magical and amazing place."
- Jennifer Gayle

What were the highlights of your week?

I AM THANKFUL FOR…   DATE:

1. _____
2. _____
3. _____

I AM THANKFUL FOR…   DATE:

1. _____
2. _____
3. _____

I AM THANKFUL FOR…   DATE:

1. _____
2. _____
3. _____

What were the highlights of your week?

I AM THANKFUL FOR...   DATE:

1. _____

2. _____

3. _____

I AM THANKFUL FOR...   DATE:

1. _____

2. _____

3. _____

I AM THANKFUL FOR...   DATE:

1. _____

2. _____

3. _____

I AM THANKFUL FOR...   DATE:

1. _____

2. _____

3. _____

> "Even in the trials of life, if we have eyes to see them, we can find good things everywhere we look."
> - Joanna Gaines

What were the highlights of your week?

I AM THANKFUL FOR…   DATE:

1. _____
2. _____
3. _____

I AM THANKFUL FOR…   DATE:

1. _____
2. _____
3. _____

I AM THANKFUL FOR…   DATE:

1. _____
2. _____
3. _____

What were the highlights of your week?

I AM THANKFUL FOR...   DATE:

1. _____

2. _____

3. _____

I AM THANKFUL FOR...   DATE:

1. _____

2. _____

3. _____

I AM THANKFUL FOR...   DATE:

1. _____

2. _____

3. _____

I AM THANKFUL FOR...   DATE:

1. _____

2. _____

3. _____

> *"Feeling gratitude isn't born in us - it's something we are taught, and in turn, we teach our children."*
> - Joyce Brothers

What were the highlights of your week?

I AM THANKFUL FOR...   DATE:

1. _____
2. _____
3. _____

I AM THANKFUL FOR...   DATE:

1. _____
2. _____
3. _____

I AM THANKFUL FOR...   DATE:

1. _____
2. _____
3. _____

What were the highlights of your week?

I AM THANKFUL FOR...   DATE:

1. _____

2. _____

3. _____

I AM THANKFUL FOR...   DATE:

1. _____

2. _____

3. _____

I AM THANKFUL FOR...   DATE:

1. _____

2. _____

3. _____

I AM THANKFUL FOR...   DATE:

1. _____

2. _____

3. _____

"Gratitude enables me to fall in love with my life every."

What were the highlights of your week?

I AM THANKFUL FOR...   DATE:

1. _____

2. _____

3. _____

I AM THANKFUL FOR...   DATE:

1. _____

2. _____

3. _____

I AM THANKFUL FOR...   DATE:

1. _____

2. _____

3. _____

What were the highlights of your week?

I AM THANKFUL FOR...   DATE:

1. _____
2. _____
3. _____

I AM THANKFUL FOR...   DATE:

1. _____
2. _____
3. _____

I AM THANKFUL FOR...   DATE:

1. _____
2. _____
3. _____

I AM THANKFUL FOR...   DATE:

1. _____
2. _____
3. _____

"Be kind. Be thoughtful. Be genuine. But most of all, be thankful"

What were the highlights of your week?

I AM THANKFUL FOR…   DATE:

1. _____

2. _____

3. _____

I AM THANKFUL FOR…   DATE:

1. _____

2. _____

3. _____

I AM THANKFUL FOR…   DATE:

1. _____

2. _____

3. _____

What were the highlights of your week?

I AM THANKFUL FOR...   DATE:

1. _____

2. _____

3. _____

I AM THANKFUL FOR...   DATE:

1. _____

2. _____

3. _____

I AM THANKFUL FOR...   DATE:

1. _____

2. _____

3. _____

I AM THANKFUL FOR...   DATE:

1. _____

2. _____

3. _____

> *"No one has ever become poor by giving."*
> — Anne Frank

What were the highlights of your week?

I AM THANKFUL FOR…   DATE:

1. _____

2. _____

3. _____

I AM THANKFUL FOR…   DATE:

1. _____

2. _____

3. _____

I AM THANKFUL FOR…   DATE:

1. _____

2. _____

3. _____

What were the highlights of your week?

I AM THANKFUL FOR...   DATE:

1. _____
2. _____
3. _____

I AM THANKFUL FOR...   DATE:

1. _____
2. _____
3. _____

I AM THANKFUL FOR...   DATE:

1. _____
2. _____
3. _____

I AM THANKFUL FOR...   DATE:

1. _____
2. _____
3. _____

> "Gratitude: The quality of being thankful; readiness to show appreciation for and to return kindness."

What were the highlights of your week?

I AM THANKFUL FOR...   DATE:

1. _____

2. _____

3. _____

I AM THANKFUL FOR...   DATE:

1. _____

2. _____

3. _____

I AM THANKFUL FOR...   DATE:

1. _____

2. _____

3. _____

What were the highlights of your week?

I AM THANKFUL FOR...   DATE:

1. _____

2. _____

3. _____

I AM THANKFUL FOR...   DATE:

1. _____

2. _____

3. _____

I AM THANKFUL FOR...   DATE:

1. _____

2. _____

3. _____

I AM THANKFUL FOR...   DATE:

1. _____

2. _____

3. _____

> "Thankfulness is measured by the number of words; gratitude is measured by the nature of our actions."
> - David O. McKay

What were the highlights of your week?

I AM THANKFUL FOR…   DATE:

1. _____
2. _____
3. _____

I AM THANKFUL FOR…   DATE:

1. _____
2. _____
3. _____

I AM THANKFUL FOR…   DATE:

1. _____
2. _____
3. _____

What were the highlights of your week?

I AM THANKFUL FOR…   DATE:

1. _____
2. _____
3. _____

I AM THANKFUL FOR…   DATE:

1. _____
2. _____
3. _____

I AM THANKFUL FOR…   DATE:

1. _____
2. _____
3. _____

I AM THANKFUL FOR…   DATE:

1. _____
2. _____
3. _____

What were the highlights of your week?

I AM THANKFUL FOR...   DATE:

1. _____

2. _____

3. _____

I AM THANKFUL FOR...   DATE:

1. _____

2. _____

3. _____

I AM THANKFUL FOR...   DATE:

1. _____

2. _____

3. _____

What were the highlights of your week?

I AM THANKFUL FOR...   DATE:

1. _____
2. _____
3. _____

I AM THANKFUL FOR...   DATE:

1. _____
2. _____
3. _____

I AM THANKFUL FOR...   DATE:

1. _____
2. _____
3. _____

I AM THANKFUL FOR...   DATE:

1. _____
2. _____
3. _____

What were the highlights of your week?

I AM THANKFUL FOR...   DATE:

1. _____

2. _____

3. _____

I AM THANKFUL FOR...   DATE:

1. _____

2. _____

3. _____

I AM THANKFUL FOR...   DATE:

1. _____

2. _____

3. _____

What were the highlights of your week?

I AM THANKFUL FOR...   DATE:

1. _____
2. _____
3. _____

I AM THANKFUL FOR...   DATE:

1. _____
2. _____
3. _____

I AM THANKFUL FOR...   DATE:

1. _____
2. _____
3. _____

I AM THANKFUL FOR...   DATE:

1. _____
2. _____
3. _____

> "Gratitude helps you to grow and expand; gratitude brings joy and laughter into your life and into the lives of all those around you."   - Eileen Caddy

What were the highlights of your week?

I AM THANKFUL FOR…   DATE:

1. _____
2. _____
3. _____

I AM THANKFUL FOR…   DATE:

1. _____
2. _____
3. _____

I AM THANKFUL FOR…   DATE:

1. _____
2. _____
3. _____

What were the highlights of your week?

I AM THANKFUL FOR...   DATE:

1. _____
2. _____
3. _____

I AM THANKFUL FOR...   DATE:

1. _____
2. _____
3. _____

I AM THANKFUL FOR...   DATE:

1. _____
2. _____
3. _____

I AM THANKFUL FOR...   DATE:

1. _____
2. _____
3. _____

> "The more grateful I am, the more beauty I see"
> - Mary Davis

What were the highlights of your week?

I AM THANKFUL FOR...   DATE:

1. _____
2. _____
3. _____

I AM THANKFUL FOR...   DATE:

1. _____
2. _____
3. _____

I AM THANKFUL FOR...   DATE:

1. _____
2. _____
3. _____

What were the highlights of your week?

I AM THANKFUL FOR...   DATE:

1. _____

2. _____

3. _____

I AM THANKFUL FOR...   DATE:

1. _____

2. _____

3. _____

I AM THANKFUL FOR...   DATE:

1. _____

2. _____

3. _____

I AM THANKFUL FOR...   DATE:

1. _____

2. _____

3. _____

> "Gratitude will shift you to a higher frequency, and you will attract much better things."
> - Rhonda Byrne

What were the highlights of your week?

I AM THANKFUL FOR...   DATE:

1. _____

2. _____

3. _____

I AM THANKFUL FOR...   DATE:

1. _____

2. _____

3. _____

I AM THANKFUL FOR...   DATE:

1. _____

2. _____

3. _____

What were the highlights of your week?

I AM THANKFUL FOR...   DATE:

1. _____

2. _____

3. _____

I AM THANKFUL FOR...   DATE:

1. _____

2. _____

3. _____

I AM THANKFUL FOR...   DATE:

1. _____

2. _____

3. _____

I AM THANKFUL FOR...   DATE:

1. _____

2. _____

3. _____

> "Got no checkbooks, got no banks, still I'd like to express my thanks. I got the sun in the morning and the moon at night."   - Irving Berlin

What were the highlights of your week?

I AM THANKFUL FOR...   DATE:

1. _____

2. _____

3. _____

I AM THANKFUL FOR...   DATE:

1. _____

2. _____

3. _____

I AM THANKFUL FOR...   DATE:

1. _____

2. _____

3. _____

What were the highlights of your week?

I AM THANKFUL FOR...   DATE:

1. _____

2. _____

3. _____

I AM THANKFUL FOR...   DATE:

1. _____

2. _____

3. _____

I AM THANKFUL FOR...   DATE:

1. _____

2. _____

3. _____

I AM THANKFUL FOR...   DATE:

1. _____

2. _____

3. _____

> "We can only be said to be alive in those moments when our hearts are conscious of our treasures."
> - Thornton Wilder

What were the highlights of your week?

I AM THANKFUL FOR…   DATE:

1. _____

2. _____

3. _____

I AM THANKFUL FOR…   DATE:

1. _____

2. _____

3. _____

I AM THANKFUL FOR…   DATE:

1. _____

2. _____

3. _____

What were the highlights of your week?

I AM THANKFUL FOR…   DATE:

1. _____

2. _____

3. _____

I AM THANKFUL FOR…   DATE:

1. _____

2. _____

3. _____

I AM THANKFUL FOR…   DATE:

1. _____

2. _____

3. _____

I AM THANKFUL FOR…   DATE:

1. _____

2. _____

3. _____

> *"Gratitude and attitude are not challenges; they are choices."*
> — Robert Braathe

What were the highlights of your week?

I AM THANKFUL FOR…   DATE:

1. _____
2. _____
3. _____

I AM THANKFUL FOR…   DATE:

1. _____
2. _____
3. _____

I AM THANKFUL FOR…   DATE:

1. _____
2. _____
3. _____

What were the highlights of your week?

I AM THANKFUL FOR...   DATE:

1. _____

2. _____

3. _____

I AM THANKFUL FOR...   DATE:

1. _____

2. _____

3. _____

I AM THANKFUL FOR...   DATE:

1. _____

2. _____

3. _____

I AM THANKFUL FOR...   DATE:

1. _____

2. _____

3. _____

> "Appreciation can make a day, even change a life. Your willingness to put it into words is all that is necessary."
> - Margaret Cousins

What were the highlights of your week?

I AM THANKFUL FOR...   DATE:

1. _____

2. _____

3. _____

I AM THANKFUL FOR...   DATE:

1. _____

2. _____

3. _____

I AM THANKFUL FOR...   DATE:

1. _____

2. _____

3. _____

What were the highlights of your week?

I AM THANKFUL FOR...   DATE:

1. _____
2. _____
3. _____

I AM THANKFUL FOR...   DATE:

1. _____
2. _____
3. _____

I AM THANKFUL FOR...   DATE:

1. _____
2. _____
3. _____

I AM THANKFUL FOR...   DATE:

1. _____
2. _____
3. _____

> "Let us be grateful to the people who make us happy; they are the charming gardeners who make our souls blossom."
> - Marcel Proust

What were the highlights of your week?

I AM THANKFUL FOR...   DATE:

1. _____

2. _____

3. _____

I AM THANKFUL FOR...   DATE:

1. _____

2. _____

3. _____

I AM THANKFUL FOR...   DATE:

1. _____

2. _____

3. _____

What were the highlights of your week?

I AM THANKFUL FOR...   DATE:

1. _____
2. _____
3. _____

I AM THANKFUL FOR...   DATE:

1. _____
2. _____
3. _____

I AM THANKFUL FOR...   DATE:

1. _____
2. _____
3. _____

I AM THANKFUL FOR...   DATE:

1. _____
2. _____
3. _____

> "We must find time to stop and thank the people who make a difference in our lives."
> - John F. Kennedy

What were the highlights of your week?

I AM THANKFUL FOR…   DATE:

1. _____
2. _____
3. _____

I AM THANKFUL FOR…   DATE:

1. _____
2. _____
3. _____

I AM THANKFUL FOR…   DATE:

1. _____
2. _____
3. _____

What were the highlights of your week?

I AM THANKFUL FOR…   DATE:

1. _____
2. _____
3. _____

I AM THANKFUL FOR…   DATE:

1. _____
2. _____
3. _____

I AM THANKFUL FOR…   DATE:

1. _____
2. _____
3. _____

I AM THANKFUL FOR…   DATE:

1. _____
2. _____
3. _____

www.ingramcontent.com/pod-product-compliance
Lightning Source LLC
Chambersburg PA
CBHW080627030426
42336CB00018B/3103